AF270513

CLIMATE CHANGE

BY CARLA MOONEY

Essential Library

An Imprint of Abdo Publishing
abdobooks.com

ABDOBOOKS.COM

Published by Abdo Publishing, a division of ABDO, PO Box 398166, Minneapolis, Minnesota 55439. Copyright © 2025 by Abdo Consulting Group, Inc. International copyrights reserved in all countries. No part of this book may be reproduced in any form without written permission from the publisher. Essential Library™ is a trademark and logo of Abdo Publishing.

Printed in the United States of America, North Mankato, Minnesota.

052024
092024

Cover Photo: Scott Book/Shutterstock Images
Interior Photos: Scott Eisen/Getty Images News/Getty Images, 4; Kylie Cooper/Getty Images News/Getty Images, 6–7; Shutterstock Images, 10, 12, 15, 41, 44, 51, 56, 60, 62, 66, 70–71, 72, 78, 81, 94, 100, 101; Karen Ford Photo/Shutterstock Images, 18–19; STR/NurPhoto/Getty Images, 22; Stock Montage/Archive Photos/Getty Images, 24; Pictorial Press Ltd/Alamy, 26; Science Source, 27; Sean Gallup/Getty Images News/Getty Images, 32; James Marvin Phelps/Shutterstock Images, 34; Diyana Dimitrova/Shutterstock Images, 36; Terray Sylvester/VWPics/AP Images, 43; Lev Radin/Pacific Press/LightRocket/Getty Images, 49; Mike Kemp/In Pictures/Getty Images, 54–55; Citizens of the Planet/Education Images/Universal Images Group/Getty Images, 65; Simon Maina/AFP/Getty Images, 77; Ina Fassbender/AFP/Getty Images, 85; Brian Inganga/AP Images, 88–89; Diana Vucane/Shutterstock Images, 90; LightField Studios/Shutterstock Images, 98

Editor: Haley Williams
Series Designer: Cynthia Della-Rovere

Library of Congress Control Number: 2023949476

PUBLISHER'S CATALOGING-IN-PUBLICATION DATA
Names: Mooney, Carla, author.
Title: Climate change / by Carla Mooney
Description: Minneapolis, Minnesota: Abdo Publishing, 2025 | Series: Protecting our planet | Includes online resources and index.
Identifiers: ISBN 9781098293420 (lib. bdg.) | ISBN 9798384912699 (ebook)
Subjects: LCSH: Climatic changes--Juvenile literature. | Global warming--Juvenile literature. | Atmospheric greenhouse effect--Juvenile literature. | Air quality--Management--Juvenile literature. | Environmental sciences--Juvenile literature.
Classification: DDC 333.951--dc23

CONTENTS

A massive amount of rain fell in Vermont between July 10 and 11, 2023. It caused the worst rain-related damage the state had experienced since 1927.

CHAPTER 1

FLOODWATERS RISING

Amelia sat in her bedroom and stared out the window. It had started raining the night before in central Vermont. Rain fell throughout the night, and by the following day, the water had carved pathways in her family's dirt driveway. While walking her dog that morning, Amelia noticed that the culvert near the end of her driveway, which usually drained excess water into the Middlebury River, was almost overflowing. Any more water and the road would start flooding.

The ground was already saturated with water. For the past month, it seemed to be raining all the time. Parts of Vermont were receiving 300 percent more rain than was usual during the summer months.[1] Amelia wondered how much more water the soil could take.

As she watched the rain from her window, one of the trees in the yard suddenly fell, barely missing the power line that brought electricity to her home. The soil had become so soggy it could no longer support the tree. "Lucky that didn't hit the house," Amelia thought.

ROADS CLOSED, RIVERS RISING

Amelia walked downstairs to the family room, where her parents watched the news from the sofa. Neither had gone to work that day because their offices did not have power. Although her house still had power, many other places did not. And with so much rain, the rivers in the area were rising fast, leading to flooding that blocked roads.

"I just got off the phone with Grandma Betty," Amelia's mom said. "Her power is out, but otherwise, she's okay." Grandma Betty lived about an hour away from Amelia's family.

"Why doesn't she just come here?" Amelia asked. "We've got power."

In some parts of Vermont, floodwater was so deep that people used kayaks to get around their town.

Her dad shook his head. "It's too dangerous right now to be on the roads," he said. "With all the rain, there's so much flooding. Emergency officials have recommended that everyone shelter in place."

By that night, rivers across Vermont had risen even higher. Many roads across the state were closed, trapping people in their homes. Hundreds of people had to evacuate their homes to escape rising floodwaters. The US National Guard used helicopters to help evacuate people who could not be reached via road.

After two days of heavy downpour, the rain finally slowed. On July 10 and 11, as much as nine inches (23 cm) of rain dumped

on parts of Vermont.[2] The damage was done, and the rivers continued to rise. In some towns, water flooded the downtown areas and rose several feet up the sides of buildings. Homes and businesses in Vermont's capital, Montpelier, experienced flooding after the nearby Winooski River overflowed its banks.

DAMAGE LEFT BEHIND

Amelia met her friend Liam in town a few days after the waters receded and the roads opened. They were shocked at the damage the flooding had left behind. Parts of some roads were broken into chunks. Debris littered the town's streets, sidewalks, and open spaces. A layer of river mud seemed to cover everything in sight.

Liam shook his head. "I don't think I've ever seen so much rain," he said.

Amelia agreed. "I was watching the news last night, and they interviewed a scientist about the rain and climate change," she said. The scientist had explained that the extreme rain Vermont had just witnessed was one of the impacts of climate change. Extreme weather events such as the historic rains in Vermont were expected to become more common in the northeastern United States and other parts of the world due to climate change.

Amelia explained that according to scientists, warmer global temperatures increase the amount of water that evaporates into the atmosphere from the ocean and other large bodies of water. This increases the water vapor in the atmosphere. When weather conditions are right, storms turn the increased water vapor into heavier rain or snow. When heavy rain falls all at once, it overwhelms a region. Rivers, streams, and lakes overflow. Soil cannot absorb that much water in such a short time. "The excess water has nowhere to go and turns into a flood," Amelia said.

"That's terrible," Liam said. "What can we do to help clean up this mess?"

Amelia pointed to a group of people clearing debris from an elementary school playground. "Let's start there," she said.

Flash Floods

Flash floods begin within six hours of heavy rainfall. The intensity of the rain and where it falls affect where flash floods happen. Urban areas are often at high risk of flash floods because they have surfaces such as concrete that do not let water pass through. Instead, the water flows to and collects in lower elevations. Flash floods are dangerous because they happen very fast and with little warning. Floodwaters may rise quickly and trap people in homes, businesses, or vehicles. The water may rise so quickly people do not have a chance to protect their property from damage.

CLEANUP EFFORTS

For several hours, the two teens worked with other community members to clean the school and playground. They picked up debris across the playground and carried it to growing piles near the curb. They also helped sweep dirt from the school floors, carried out ruined items, and helped teachers find what could be salvaged from their water-soaked classrooms. By the end of the day, Amelia and Liam were exhausted. But they agreed to meet the next day to help with more cleanup work in town.

That night, Amelia and her family decided to make an emergency plan for the next time extreme weather hit their area.

They gathered water, food, batteries, medication, and other critical supplies for an emergency kit. They also picked a meeting place and figured out how they would contact each other if they were separated in an emergency.

Before bed, Amelia opened her laptop and searched the internet for information about extreme weather and climate change. She read an article about a Pennsylvania program that tested how well battery-powered school buses performed compared with traditional fossil fuel–powered ones. Using battery-powered vehicles instead of those fueled by gasoline reduces the amount of greenhouse gases released into the air, which can help slow climate change and the extreme weather it causes.

Immediately, Amelia emailed her local school board and attached a link to the school bus article. Her community was already feeling the effects of climate change. She wanted to be part of the solution.

The troposphere, which is the lowest part of Earth's atmosphere, is where most of the planet's weather occurs.

THE SCIENCE OF CLIMATE CHANGE

Some people use the words *climate* and *weather* interchangeably. However, these words do not mean the same thing. Weather is what happens in the atmosphere each day. This could be whether an area is sunny or rainy, hot or cold, or windy or humid. Weather can sometimes change very quickly. For example, in a given area, it might be raining in the morning and sunny in the afternoon. Weather also varies in different locations worldwide. On any given day, the weather in Iceland is different from the weather in Kenya.

Climate is the usual long-term weather pattern of an area. It can vary in different places. For example, Florida typically has mild, wet winters while Maine has cold, snowy winters. Climate can also vary from season to season in the same place. An area's summer climate may be very different from its winter one. Earth's climate is a combination of all the regional climates worldwide.

Various factors can cause the planet's climate to change, such as when average temperatures increase or decrease or when rainfall amounts go up or down. While weather changes daily, climate change is much slower. It can take thousands of years for the climate to change.

SIGNS OF CLIMATE CHANGE

Technology such as satellites, weather stations, and radars collect climate information worldwide. This data, collected over many years, shows that Earth's climate is changing rapidly. One strong piece of evidence of climate change is the rising of Earth's average surface temperatures. Since the late 1800s, global temperatures have risen about two degrees Fahrenheit (1°C). Most of that warming has occurred since the late 1900s. In fact, 2016 and 2023 are the two warmest years on record, according to scientists at the World Meteorological Organization.[1] As Earth's temperature rises, its oceans are also getting warmer. In every decade since around 1970, the top part of the ocean has warmed approximately 0.2 degrees Fahrenheit (0.1°C).[2]

Since 1880, the surface temperature of Earth has increased by an average of 0.14 degrees Fahrenheit (0.08°C) per decade.[3]

As Earth's atmosphere and oceans warm, ice sheets and glaciers are shrinking. Measurements have shown that ice sheets in both Greenland and Antarctica have gotten smaller. Glaciers worldwide are shrinking as less ice accumulates or more ice melts. Arctic sea ice is also declining. Snow cover across the Northern Hemisphere is shrinking as well, and warmer temperatures have caused snow to start melting earlier in the year.

The melting of glacial ice and ice sheets causes sea levels to rise. Research shows that the worldwide sea level has risen about eight inches (20 cm) since the early 1900s.[4] Since the early 2000s, the ocean has been rising even faster. All these signs are evidence of Earth's changing climate.

CAUSES OF CLIMATE CHANGE

Some changes in the climate are natural. Throughout the planet's history, Earth's climate has constantly been changing. There have been times when the planet's climate has been warmer or colder. In the past, most of these instances were caused by tiny changes in Earth's orbit, which moved the planet closer to or farther away from the sun and its warmth. Other natural events, such as volcanic eruptions and landmass changes, have also affected Earth's climate.

How Volcanoes Affect the Climate

Volcanic eruptions can sometimes cool or warm Earth's climate. When a volcano erupts, it sends volcanic gases and ash into the atmosphere. While ash quickly falls to Earth's surface, volcanic gases can linger in the atmosphere. Gases such as sulfur dioxide can form fine sulfate aerosols. These tiny particles hang in the air and reflect the sun's radiation into space, cooling Earth's atmosphere. Huge volcanic eruptions can also send large amounts of carbon dioxide into the atmosphere, where it can contribute to global warming.

However, scientists believe natural events are not causing Earth's current warming trend. Instead, evidence suggests that human activity is causing these changes in climate. During the Industrial Revolution that began in the mid-1700s, people started building factories and railroads to manufacture and transport goods. In today's world, people drive cars and fly airplanes. Houses are now heated and cooled with furnaces and air conditioners. And many appliances, from refrigerators to computers, are powered by electricity. These activities all require energy. That energy usually comes from burning fossil fuels, such as oil, coal, and gas.

GREENHOUSE GASES

Burning fossil fuels releases greenhouse gases, particularly carbon dioxide, into Earth's atmosphere. Fossil fuels are made from the buried remains of dead plants and animals, which contain large amounts of carbon. When fossil fuels are burned, that carbon is released into the atmosphere as carbon dioxide gas.

In Earth's atmosphere, greenhouse gases include water vapor, carbon dioxide, methane, and nitrous oxide. These gases trap heat in the atmosphere. As the sun shines through Earth's atmosphere during the day, the planet's surface warms. At night, Earth's surface cools and releases heat back into the atmosphere. Greenhouse gases trap some heat near the planet's surface. This process helps Earth stay at a constant, livable temperature.

Greenhouse gases also absorb heat energy released by Earth's surface, bodies of water, and air. They radiate heat in all directions. Some heat energy radiates back to Earth, warming the surface and lower atmosphere even more. It adds to the heat that the atmosphere and surface absorb from sunlight.

Greenhouse gases release absorbed heat energy slowly, similar to how fireplace bricks release heat long after the fire is out. As more greenhouse gases accumulate in Earth's atmosphere, more heat releases from the planet's surface and is absorbed by the greenhouse gases. The heat then radiates back to the surface, which causes Earth's surface temperature to rise.

Earth's Atmosphere

Earth's atmosphere is a layer of gases that surrounds the planet. This layer is made mostly of nitrogen and oxygen. Other gases, including argon, carbon dioxide, neon, helium, and hydrogen, are present in smaller quantities. The atmosphere is like a blanket that insulates and protects Earth. It absorbs and holds the sun's heat, which helps keep Earth warm. This process keeps the planet's temperature stable, making it suitable for life.

Human activity has been responsible for almost all the increase in greenhouse gases in the atmosphere. In the United States in 2021, the largest source of greenhouse gas emissions was burning fossil fuels for transportation at 28 percent. The other top sources of emissions that year were electricity production at 25 percent and industry at 23 percent.[5]

WARMING FASTER

Although Earth's climate constantly changes, the current rate
of warming is happening much faster than at any other time
in history. When Earth warmed after past ice ages, the global
temperature rose between 7.2 and 12.6 degrees Fahrenheit
(4–7°C) during a period of about 5,000 years. However, in the

past 100 years, Earth's temperature has risen around 1.3 degrees Fahrenheit (0.7°C). This increase is about ten times faster than previous warming events.[6]

Since 1981, the rate of increase in global temperatures has more than doubled.[7] Global annual temperatures have risen by 0.32 degrees Fahrenheit (0.18°C) per decade. As a result, Earth is hotter than ever. Through 2023, the nine warmest years on record have occurred since 2015. The warmest year ever recorded was 2023, and the second- and third-warmest years were in 2016 and 2020.[8]

> We're the first generation to see the effects of climate change, and the last generation who can do anything about it.[9]
>
> —Michael McGinn, former mayor of Seattle, Washington, 2013

Scientists believe that the current rapid warming of Earth cannot be explained by natural causes. Instead, human activities are the primary driver of the planet's recent warming. Burning increasing amounts of fossil fuels releases more greenhouse gases into the atmosphere. These gases trap heat energy and further warm Earth's atmosphere and surface.

At the same time, humans have cleared forests to build houses, factories, and roads. Trees absorb carbon dioxide from the air, helping keep the amount of this gas in the atmosphere in check. As more forests are cut down, though, there are fewer trees to absorb carbon dioxide. The level of carbon dioxide in the atmosphere then rises.

CLIMATE CHANGE AFFECTS EVERYONE

Scientists predict that Earth's warming will continue in the coming years. Stanford University in California and Colorado State University researchers used artificial intelligence (AI) to predict future warming timelines. Their study, published in 2023, predicted that by the 2030s Earth's temperature will rise more than 2.7 degrees Fahrenheit (1.5°C) above pre-industrial levels, which are the global temperature levels from 1850 to 1900. The study also predicted that if greenhouse gas emissions remain high, Earth has a 50 percent chance of becoming 3.6 degrees Fahrenheit (2°C) hotter than pre-industrial averages by 2050. And by 2060, the study predicted a more than 80 percent chance that level will be reached.[10]

Earth's rapid rate of warming is sparking climate change that affects every living creature. As surface temperature rises, more snow and ice will melt. Oceans will continue rising. Some areas will experience hotter temperatures, while others will have colder winters. Extreme weather events such as hurricanes, heat waves,

Past Evidence

Scientists learn about past climates by examining evidence found in nature. Tree rings, glacier ice, sedimentary rocks, ocean sediment, and coral reefs all hold clues about Earth's climate hundreds of thousands of years ago. For example, tiny air bubbles from the past are stuck in glacial ice. Scientists can analyze the air in these bubbles to learn what the atmosphere used to be like long ago. With this information, scientists can build a record of the planet's past climates.

GRETA THUNBERG

Greta Thunberg is an environmental activist from Stockholm, Sweden. As a young girl, Thunberg learned about climate change and persuaded her parents to make changes in their lifestyle to lower their carbon emissions. Among other changes, she and her parents gave up eating meat and stopped traveling on planes.

In 2018, 15-year-old Thunberg demonstrated outside Sweden's parliament to protest and bring attention to climate change. She held a sign that said, "School Strike for Climate." News of Thunberg's activism quickly spread around the world. She encouraged other students to join her protests, which led to a school climate strike movement called Fridays for Future.

Thunberg also began giving speeches to urge world leaders to take action against climate change. At the 2019 World Economic Forum in Switzerland, she warned the audience, saying, "Our house is on fire."[11] She urged the audience to take action against climate change. Today, Thunberg continues to work to raise awareness about climate change.

In 2019, Greta Thunberg became the youngest person to be named *Time* magazine's "Person of the Year" at 16 years old.

droughts, and floods will become more common. Animals and plants will have to adapt to habitat changes or be forced to migrate. Certain diseases may become more common in animals, plants, and humans.

People worldwide are already experiencing the effects of climate change. And if the world cannot find a way to reduce emissions and slow global warming, climate change will cause even more problems. In the western United States, droughts and disappearing glaciers will lead to more water shortages and an increased risk of wildfires. Coastal regions in the eastern and southeastern United States will battle more flooding as sea levels rise. Forests, farms, and cities will experience heat waves, heavy rainfall, increased flooding, and new pests.

All these factors can heavily damage and destroy crops and fisheries. Disruptions to agriculture may cause food shortages. Temperature changes, precipitation changes, and flooding will change habitats, which can cause the extinction of animal and plant species. And allergies, asthma, and infectious diseases will affect more people as climate changes make more regions favorable to pollen-producing plants, pollution, and disease-causing pathogens.

Joseph Fourier was born on March 21, 1768, in Auxerre, France.

THE HISTORY OF CLIMATE CHANGE

As early as the 1800s, scientists predicted global warming. French mathematician and physicist Joseph Fourier was fascinated with understanding how Earth maintained its temperature. Fourier theorized that there must be a certain amount of energy going into and out of the planet for it to maintain its temperature. But after his calculations, he discovered that Earth was warmer than it should have been at the time.

With his findings, Fourier believed that Earth's atmosphere was somehow holding heat close to the planet's surface. In 1824, Fourier wrote a paper suggesting atmospheric gases might be creating a barrier to trap heat near Earth's surface. This idea later became known as the greenhouse effect.

In 1837, Fourier wrote another paper explaining how after some time, the amount of heat in the atmosphere could change because of natural causes and human actions. It was one of the first times someone had predicted that Earth's climate could change. However, there were still no answers as to how that change occurred.

EARLY EXPERIMENTS

In the mid-1850s, a better understanding of how atmospheric gases trapped heat began to emerge. In 1856, amateur scientist Eunice Newton Foote experimented on how different gases could trap heat. Foote placed glass cylinders filled with different gases under sunlight to heat them and then would move the cylinders into the shade. She used thermometers to measure how the temperatures of the gases changed.

Eunice Newton Foote is considered a pioneer for both climate science and women's rights.

During her experiment, Foote discovered that the cylinders with carbon dioxide and water vapor got hotter in the sun and stayed hotter longer in the shade than cylinders of moist and dry air did. Her experiment showed that those gases trapped heat. That same year, Foote wrote an article about her experiment and predicted the potential impact her findings could have on Earth. She wrote, "An atmosphere of that gas would give to our earth a high temperature."[1]

In 1859 and 1860, Irish scientist John Tyndall also tested gases and their heat-trapping capacity. Like Foote, Tyndall found that water vapor and carbon dioxide trapped more heat than dry air.

His experiments showed carbon dioxide was especially good at retaining heat and could trap up to 1,000 times more heat than regular air.[2]

FIRST CLIMATE MODELS

Building on earlier scientific discoveries, Swedish physicist Svante Arrhenius developed a mathematical understanding of climate change in 1896. Arrhenius was interested in what caused Earth's past ice ages. Some scientists believed changes in Earth's orbit caused the ice ages. Others theorized atmospheric changes were the cause, including varied carbon dioxide levels. Arrhenius believed atmospheric changes made more sense, so he set out to prove it.

Using data from other scientists, Arrhenius calculated how much heat would be trapped in the atmosphere if carbon dioxide and water vapor levels changed. The work was tedious, with Arrhenius spending months making thousands of calculations by hand. In the end, he made a prediction that twice the amount of carbon dioxide in the atmosphere would cause Earth's temperature to rise by 9 to 10.8 degrees Fahrenheit (5–6°C).[3]

Svante Arrhenius received a Nobel Prize in Chemistry in 1903. He was the third person to receive the award.

Arrhenius and others did not worry about short-term global warming or the effect of industrialization on Earth's climate. They did not think burning fossil fuels would reach a level that would cause significant change. Instead, Arrhenius predicted it would take more than 3,000 years for carbon dioxide levels to rise by 50 percent.[4]

EARLY WARNINGS

In 1938, British engineer Guy Callendar collected weather data from almost 150 weather stations worldwide. Callendar used the data to calculate global temperature trends. He found that during the past 50 years, temperatures around the world had risen 0.5 degrees Fahrenheit (0.3°C).[5] Callendar believed that carbon dioxide emissions from burning fossil fuels had caused the increased temperatures. However, many scientists ignored Callendar's work, believing human activity couldn't significantly affect Earth's climate.

Two decades later in 1958, geochemist Charles David Keeling conducted a study to measure the amount of carbon dioxide in the air. Keeling traveled to a weather observatory on the Mauna Loa volcano in Hawaii and to an observatory at the South Pole. While at those locations, he measured carbon dioxide levels in the atmosphere every day. By the end of the 1960s, he had proof that carbon dioxide levels were rising. Keeling analyzed the carbon dioxide in the samples and eventually linked the gas's rising levels to burning fossil fuels.

In the early days, studying Earth's climate was often tedious work, as scientists had to do many mathematical calculations by hand. That changed in 1967. Scientists Syukuro Manabe and Richard Wetherald created the first computer model of Earth's climate.

The model incorporated many climate factors, including atmosphere, clouds, and oceans. It allowed researchers to more clearly see how increased carbon dioxide levels affected Earth's surface temperatures. Manabe and Wetherald's model calculated that if atmospheric carbon dioxide doubled, the result would cause global temperatures to rise by about 3.6 degrees Fahrenheit (2°C).[6]

In 1968, glaciologist John Mercer warned that Earth's warming climate could seriously affect the planet's ice sheets and sea levels. That year in West Antarctica, Mercer discovered evidence that a freshwater lake had once existed there. Mercer believed his discovery proved that the West Antarctic Ice Sheet had once melted entirely, something that scientists had previously believed not to be possible. Mercer warned that it could potentially happen again as Earth's oceans warmed and caused the ice

Glacier Loss

Glaciers worldwide have been melting, which is a sign of climate change. A glacier is a large accumulation of snow, ice, and rock over many years. At higher elevations, snow builds and eventually gets compacted into ice. At lower elevations, some glacier ice naturally melts and breaks off. To understand what is happening to glaciers worldwide, scientists at the World Glacier Monitoring Service have followed a sample of about 40 glaciers. In 2020, they released a report on glacier change that showed evidence of melting. The scientists discovered that between 1970 and 2020, the studied glaciers had lost a significant amount of ice, an amount that was equal to cutting off 90.2 feet (27.5 m) of ice from the top of each glacier.[7]

sheets to melt. He also predicted that melting ice sheets would cause sea levels to rise. Years later, some of Mercer's warning would come true. Beginning in 1995, parts of the Antarctic's Larsen Ice Shelf began to collapse from increased global temperatures.

THE IPCC

As evidence of climate change and its impact began to accumulate, people worldwide started to pay more attention. In 1988, the United Nations (UN) created the Intergovernmental Panel on Climate Change (IPCC) to review and report on the scientific study of climate change. The IPCC's goal was to provide a clear picture of what scientists had discovered about climate change and its potential impacts on the environment and society.

In 1990, the IPCC released its First Assessment Report. This report later led to the creation of a treaty known as the UN Framework Convention on Climate Change (UNFCCC), which was officially enforced beginning in 1994. The UNFCCC was the first global treaty to address climate change. As part of this treaty, participating countries agreed to take steps to reduce global warming and implement measures to handle the consequences of climate change. Over the next few decades, the IPCC released numerous reports on climate change.

GLOBAL AGREEMENT

Faced with scientific evidence of climate change, governments worldwide agreed that something must be done to reduce greenhouse gas emissions and slow global warming. They debated how to fight climate change, who was responsible, and how to set and track emission-reduction goals. The UNFCCC created an annual forum to discuss efforts to stabilize the level of greenhouse gases in the atmosphere. These yearly meetings led to future global climate change agreements.

The Kyoto Protocol was the world's first legally binding climate treaty. It was adopted in 1997 and was officially enforced starting in 2005. In this treaty, developed countries had to commit to reducing their greenhouse gas emissions between 2008 and 2012 by an average of 5 percent below the levels from 1990.[8] The treaty also established a system to monitor each country's progress. However, it did not force developing countries to

> The climate emergency is a race we are losing, but it is a race we can win.[9]
>
> —António Guterres,
> UN Secretary-General, 2019

The UN has held a Climate Change Conference almost every year since 1995. COP27, the 2022 conference, took place in Sharm el-Sheikh, Egypt.

reduce emissions. Among those exempt were China and India, which are both significant emissions producers.

The Paris Agreement was adopted in 2015 to build on and eventually replace the Kyoto Protocol. It was put into full effect in late 2016. This agreement requires all participating countries to submit an emissions-reduction plan. Each government sets targets with the overall goal of preventing Earth's average temperature from rising 3.6 degrees Fahrenheit (2°C) above pre-industrial levels.[10]

Countries are responsible for evaluating their progress toward their goals. The Paris Agreement also aims to achieve net-zero emissions globally before 2100. Net-zero emissions occur when greenhouse gas emissions equal the amount of greenhouse gases removed from the atmosphere.

Meanwhile, life on Earth has increasingly felt the effects of climate change. Extreme weather events, intense heat waves, droughts, rising sea levels, and changing precipitation patterns have impacted people, animals, and plants worldwide. Climate scientists believe that the world's response to climate change should incorporate several solutions, from changing how people use energy to restoring Earth's natural climate defenses.

Coal produces the most carbon dioxide emissions of any fossil fuel.

REPLACING FOSSIL FUELS

The evidence that human activity, mainly burning fossil fuels, causes climate change is mounting. Therefore, the single most significant step people can take to battle climate change is reducing the use of fossil fuels. Today, burning coal, oil, and natural gas worldwide is responsible for most greenhouse gas emissions. According to the UN, fossil fuels are the source of more than 75 percent of greenhouse gas emissions and almost 90 percent of carbon dioxide emissions worldwide.[1] To replace fossil fuels, new energy sources are needed.

FOSSIL FUELS

Fossil fuels such as coal, oil, and natural gas are the most commonly used energy sources today. They were created deep under Earth's surface by heat and pressure over the course of millions of years. Fossil fuels are removed from the ground by drilling or mining. These fuels are nonrenewable resources. Currently, people are using fossil fuels much faster than they can be created under Earth's surface.

Unlike fossil fuels, renewable energy sources are replenished naturally. Sunlight and wind are two examples of renewable energy sources. Renewable energy also produces much lower emission levels than burning fossil fuels. Replacing fossil fuels with renewable energy sources is one way to reduce emissions and slow climate change.

SOLAR ENERGY

Solar energy is one of the most plentiful energy resources worldwide. Solar energy comes from the sun. The energy that comes from sunlight can be turned into electricity, provide light, and heat water. In 2022, the solar industry generated about 3.4 percent of electricity in the United States.[2]

In the Northern Hemisphere, solar panels are usually placed facing true south so they can receive the most direct sunlight during the day.

Solar energy is collected using three main technologies. These are photovoltaics, solar heating and cooling, and concentrating solar power (CSP). Photovoltaic devices generate electricity from sunlight using semiconductors. Light causes electrons in the semiconductors to move through an electrical circuit. It generates electricity that can power electrical devices, be sent into an electrical grid, or be stored in batteries for later use.

Photovoltaic devices can generate electricity to power anything from phone chargers to entire buildings. Solar panels on roofs or on the ground are made from many photovoltaic cells working together. These panels do not emit greenhouse gases or other pollutants as they generate electricity, and they continue working year-round as long as the sun is shining.

Solar heating and cooling systems collect energy from the sun. These systems use the energy to heat, cool, and provide hot water to homes, businesses, and industries. For example, solar water heating systems use a collector to gather heat from the sun. They then transfer the heat to safe drinking water. The heated water flows from the collector to a hot water tank and can be used as needed.

CSP plants use mirrors to focus sunlight and create extremely high temperatures. That heat is then stored and used to run electricity-producing turbines and engines. Because they can store heat, CSP plants can generate electricity as needed, whether it's day or night.

WIND ENERGY

Wind energy uses the power of the wind to generate electricity using a wind turbine. The most common types of wind turbines have two or three long, thin blades, making them look like airplane propellers. Wind moves the turbine's blades, which are attached to a rotor, and then the rotor spins a generator, creating electricity. Electricity produced by wind turbines can be used immediately, connected to the electrical grid, or stored for later use.

Wind turbines can produce electricity even when it is cloudy or rainy. Scientists are working on ways to better store electricity produced by wind energy. In 2022, wind energy produced about 10.2 percent of the United States' electricity.[3]

OTHER ALTERNATIVE ENERGY SOURCES

In addition to solar and wind energy, several other renewable energy sources can be part of a solution to replace fossil fuels. Geothermal energy comes from natural heat under Earth's surface. It is considered renewable energy because the planet continuously produces heat. Geothermal power plants drill below Earth's surface to use steam from deep hot water reservoirs. The steam rotates a turbine to generate electricity. Geothermal energy can also be used to heat and cool buildings. A system of underground pipes is used to pump a water mixture through the building. The mixture absorbs heat stored underground and carries it to heat pumps, where it is concentrated and used to send warm air throughout a building.

Renewable energy sources accounted for about 21 percent of the United States' total electricity generation from power plants in 2022.[4]

Hydropower uses the energy of water as it moves from higher to lower elevations. It can be generated from stored water in a reservoir or from the flow of a river. Hydropower is one of the largest sources of renewable energy electricity. However, it requires people to build significant infrastructure, which

Although hydropower is a quickly growing renewable energy source, it can also cause environmental problems. An artificial reservoir can greatly change the environment and rivers where it is built. For example, dams and reservoirs reduce and block river flows, disrupting the plants, fish, and other organisms that live there. Slower water flow can increase water temperatures, which can affect temperature-sensitive organisms. Dams and slower water flows can also cause sediment to accumulate along the dam and riverbed, trapping heavy metals and other pollutants. These consequences often harm the ecosystem and the local fish, birds, and other wildlife.

can negatively affect the environment and disrupt rivers and ecosystems. Smaller-scale hydropower technologies are believed to be more environmentally friendly.

Scientists are also studying the potential of new technologies to harness energy from the ocean's movement. Ocean energy can be generated from waves, tides, currents, and different ocean temperatures. For example, wave energy converters generate electricity from the ocean's surface waves. In one device, wave motion acts as a piston to drive air in and out of a chamber. The moving air drives a turbine to generate electricity. Tidal energy converters are another kind of device that use the movement of tide currents to spin the propellers of underwater turbines to generate electricity.

IMPROVING ENERGY EFFICIENCY

Energy efficiency is another way to consume less of any energy resource, including fossil fuels. It uses technology to help reduce or eliminate energy waste. People can still do the same activities, but less energy is consumed overall. Energy efficiency is simply using energy in a smarter way.

Improving energy efficiency in buildings, appliances, equipment, and vehicles can have many benefits. Less energy use reduces pollution and carbon dioxide emissions. Some scientists estimate that by 2050, energy-efficient appliances, electronics, lighting, and insulation could eliminate 606 million short tons (550 million metric tons) of annual carbon pollution in the United States.[5]

Energy efficiency technologies can be used everywhere, from homes and businesses to factories and power plants. Many strategies are simple. These include weatherproofing buildings, installing cool roofs, and using LED light bulbs. Weatherproofed buildings and cool roofs keep interior temperatures stable and reduce the need for heating and cooling. LED light bulbs use less electricity than traditional incandescent light bulbs. These strategies all contribute to people using less energy.

LED light bulbs used in homes last almost 25 times longer than incandescent light bulbs.

CAMPAIGN FOR CLEAN ENERGY

For Levi Draheim, the effects of climate change have already affected his home on a barrier island off the eastern coast of Florida. For years, Levi swam, surfed, and sailed near the island's beaches. However, warming temperatures caused seaweed and harmful algae blooms to surround the island. The algae blooms and seaweed wash up on the beach and eventually rot, causing the beach to smell bad. The algae blooms have also killed native seagrass, which has led to the death of local wildlife that rely on the plants.

The island has also experienced more frequent and intense weather, including Hurricane Irma in 2017. The hurricane caused billions of dollars in damage across Florida and flooding at Levi's home. After Hurricane Irma, Levi's family left the island and moved to mainland Florida. "It's kind of disappointing not being able to live on the barrier island anymore, because there's so much fun stuff that I could do. Most of my friends, they live on the barrier island," said Levi. "It's a mix of disappointment and also frustration, frustration with leaders."[6]

When he was eight, Levi got involved with Our Children's Trust, a nonprofit law firm involved in climate action, through

> **The Constitution says that I have a right to life, liberty, and property. How am I supposed to enjoy life, liberty, and property, if one day, the island I live on will be underwater?**[7]
>
> —Levi Draheim, climate activist, 2019

Levi Draheim, *center,* was the youngest of the 21 young people who sued the federal government in 2015.

his church. In 2015, Levi joined 20 other young people across the nation to file a lawsuit that challenged the federal government's development of fossil fuels. The case argued that the development of these fuels violated people's constitutional rights to freedom, life, and property. In 2018, at ten years old, Levi joined another lawsuit with other Florida youth that challenged the state's energy system. The courts eventually dismissed both cases. But Levi did not give up.

Levi has joined other young Floridians to campaign for clean, renewable energy in their state. The group filed a petition in January 2022 that called upon the state's Department of Agriculture and Consumer Services to follow a mandatory law requiring the state to set goals to move Florida to clean energy. This time, their efforts got results. In 2022, the state announced plans to reach 100 percent clean energy by 2050.[8]

Pollution from vehicle emissions can lead people to have health issues such as asthma or lung cancer.

CHAPTER 5

SUSTAINABLE TRANSPORTATION

People use fossil fuels to power many kinds of vehicles, including cars, trucks, trains, ships, and airplanes. Transportation is one of the most significant contributors to greenhouse gas emissions worldwide. In 2021, transportation was the largest source of US emissions at 28 percent, according to the Environmental Protection Agency (EPA).[1] Eliminating emissions from the billions of vehicles across the planet is essential to reducing greenhouse gases in the atmosphere and slowing climate change.

EMISSIONS AND POLLUTION

Greenhouse gas emissions are released into the atmosphere when petroleum-based fuels, such as gasoline and diesel, are burned in a vehicle's internal combustion engine. Most of the emissions that come from vehicles are carbon dioxide. Internal combustion engines also release small amounts of the greenhouse gases methane and nitrous oxide.

In transportation, cars and trucks are two of the major sources of emissions. These vehicles contribute more than half of the emissions from transportation in the United States.[2] Other transportation emissions sources include commercial aircraft, ships, boats, and trains. Many companies are looking into ways to make these forms of transportation more environmentally friendly.

ELECTRIC VEHICLES

Making transportation more sustainable would help limit and eventually eliminate the damaging emissions and pollution produced by fossil fuel–powered vehicles. Some of the most promising sustainable transportation solutions are electric vehicles. These vehicles do not use fossil fuels to run internal combustion engines. Instead, a large battery pack supplies power to electric motors. The battery charges when plugged into a power source. Because they do not burn fossil fuels, electric vehicles do not release harmful emissions while driving.

All-electric vehicles have some drawbacks, though. First, these vehicles can be more expensive than traditional vehicles. But some of this cost can be offset by savings on fuel. Another drawback is a shorter driving range. A gas-powered car can drive farther on one tank of gas than an electric vehicle can drive on a single charge.

Several factors affect an electric car's driving range. Extreme temperatures often reduce driving range because more electricity must be used to heat or cool the interior. Driving on highways where rapid acceleration is needed also uses more energy and reduces driving range. Carrying heavy loads or driving up steep inclines can reduce an electric vehicle's range as well.

Charging electric vehicles can also be challenging. Public charging stations can be hard to find or unreliable in some areas. And when an operational charging station is available, it can take hours to charge the car's battery. However, new technologies are being developed to increase the driving range of electric vehicles and improve charging equipment. These changes seek to reduce charging speeds and increase reliability.

> We're moving in the right direction with electric cars. . . . But the question is: How fast do we get there? And, you know, if you look at what we're already seeing with climate change, we're going to have to move faster.[4]
>
> —David Reichmuth, senior engineer at the Union of Concerned Scientists, 2019

IMPROVING PUBLIC TRANSPORTATION

Reducing the number of vehicles on the road is another way to reduce transportation-based emissions and pollution. According to the University of California in Los Angeles, vehicles on the road release an average of one pound (0.5 kg) of carbon dioxide every mile.[5] Taking public transportation instead of driving private cars gets people to where they need to go while releasing fewer greenhouse gases into the atmosphere. This is because buses can hold dozens of people and trains carry hundreds of people while cars usually carry only one or two.

For people to use public transportation, it needs to be convenient. Some communities are investing in transit-oriented development to make public transit more accessible. Transit-oriented development designs communities where activities, jobs, services, and public spaces are within walking distance of or are easily accessed by public transportation. With this type of community design, it is easier for people to drive less, which lowers greenhouse gas emissions.

Since 2010, Seattle, Washington, has encouraged residents to leave their cars at home and use public transportation, bike,

In August 2023, New York opened the first buildings for its new transit-oriented development project, which included apartments, retail spaces, and public plazas all within walking distance of several train stations.

or walk to work. The city has invested in transit projects to make public transportation more convenient and affordable. It added bus routes and increased bus frequency. The city is also working on projects to expand its light rail and rapid bus transit services.

In addition to making public transit more convenient and accessible, Seattle has made it more affordable. The city's transit systems offer discounted fares for low-income and young riders. It has partnered with local corporations to encourage workers to use public transportation by paying for part of the monthly transit passes and by funding expanded service hours.

Seattle's efforts have increased public transportation use. Between 2010 and 2018, the percentage of people driving alone to work declined from 53 to 44 percent, the steepest drop in solo driving commuters in the United States. During that same period, the percentage of people riding Seattle's public transportation rose from 5 percent to 25 percent. The percentage of those who chose to walk to work rose from 3 percent to 12 percent.[6] More people also decided to bike to work or work from home. Seattle's results show that it is possible to get people to change their behavior and embrace more sustainable transportation options.

CONGESTION PRICING

Congestion pricing is another strategy some cities use to encourage people to choose more sustainable transportation. This strategy involves drivers paying a fee in order to use their cars on busy city roads during peak driving times. Congestion pricing is designed to decrease the number of cars on the road, which reduces emissions and improves air quality. At the same time, the fees generate funding that can be used to improve public transportation systems.

Congestion pricing plans are used in cities such as London, England; Stockholm, Sweden; and Singapore. These cities have reported benefits, including reduced traffic and less carbon dioxide pollution. In London, traffic congestion decreased

30 percent a year after the plan was implemented. In Stockholm, a study revealed a 50 percent decrease in doctor visits for children's asthma, a sign that air pollution had dropped.[7]

In 2023, New York City moved forward with a plan to implement congestion pricing. The Central Business District Tolling Program plan would charge drivers tolls during peak driving hours in many parts of Manhattan. The program aims to reduce traffic in Manhattan, improve air quality, and raise funding for New York's public transportation system. If successful, the plan could become a model for other cities nationwide. New York governor Kathy Hochul said:

> We are going to be the very first state in the nation, the very first city in America, to have a congestion pricing plan. . . . Others will look at us. Other cities are paying attention. How is it going to work here? Well, we're going to show them. We're going to show them how you do this.[8]

WALKING AND BIKING

Making it easier for people to walk or bike instead of driving can also reduce harmful emissions. Urban design strategies, known as 15-minute cities or complete neighborhoods, plan cities where most residents can reach all basic needs by foot or bike. Creating urban areas where people can easily bike or walk reduces commute times, congestion, emissions, and pollution.

Biking instead of driving just once a day can lower the average person's transportation-related carbon emissions by 67 percent.[9]

In Tshwane, South Africa, the city government has implemented several programs to encourage bike travel. It has designated car-free streets, hosted cycle-to-work festivals, and piloted a bike-sharing program with both standard and electric bikes. Tshwane also operates the Shova Kalula bicycle program, which provides free bicycles for people living in underprivileged communities outside the city. The program looks to improve access to bicycles and encourage biking culture.

BIKES FOR LOWER EMISSIONS

Climate activists in cities worldwide are working to increase sustainable transportation choices. In Chicago, Illinois, a group called Chicago, Bike Grid Now! is pushing for safer, bicycle-friendly routes throughout the city. The group wants 10 percent of Chicago streets to be more accessible to pedestrians and bikers. This amounts to around 450 miles (724 km) of the city's 4,500 miles (7,240 km) of streets. Only 28 miles (45 km) of those streets had protected bike lanes in 2023.[10]

In the group's proposed plan, a connected network of bike-friendly lanes would be quickly and inexpensively created around the city. The plan calls for a speed limit of ten miles per hour (16 kmh) for cars on residential streets and certain parts of commercial streets.[11] Cyclists, pedestrians, wheelchairs, and scooters would have the right of way on these streets.

Eventually, the proposed plan calls for the city to replace the temporary infrastructure with permanent infrastructure.

"The idea is we create some streets that are safe without a huge expense, and we can do that in a matter of weeks or months, not years or decades or generations," said Nate Hutcheson, cofounder of Chicago, Bike Grid Now! "We need to create something now that protects people and makes it safe to get around the city, and then improve it over time."[13]

Chicago, Bike Grid Now! has also organized bike rides and events to bring awareness to the need for safer bicycling lanes

London has many cycling routes, known as Cycleways, across the city. These routes make biking safer and make it easier for bikers to get around the city.

throughout Chicago. The organization has partnered with other sustainable transportation groups to make a call for climate action. Hutcheson said, "I'm most proud that we've created a way for all the people out there that are frustrated with the current infrastructure and the lack of progress . . . to get involved. And it's very accessible, and a lot of people have been able to join."[14]

The EPA listed Los Angeles, California, as the US city with the most certified energy-efficient buildings in 2023.

SUSTAINABLE BUILDINGS

The energy used to keep buildings running makes them a significant source of carbon emissions throughout the world. From construction to demolition, buildings use energy, water, and raw materials. Buildings also generate waste and produce harmful emissions. They can damage land and habitats where they stand. Sustainable design aims to create buildings that conserve resources, minimize emissions and waste, and do little harm to the environment.

ENERGY-EFFICIENT TECHNOLOGIES

One of the simplest ways to make a building more sustainable is to incorporate energy-efficient technologies. Energy-efficient buildings integrate renewable energy sources into different parts of the building. Common energy-efficient technologies include solar panels, insulation, appliances, automated lighting, smart meters, automation systems, and programmable thermostats. Each of these technologies can reduce the energy used by buildings and reduce harmful emissions.

Retrofitting

Sometimes, sustainable building design involves retrofitting existing buildings rather than building new ones. Retrofitting is when new materials or technologies are added to an existing structure. It can be more sustainable and less expensive to retrofit a structure than to build a new one. Retrofitting existing buildings also has less of an impact on the surrounding environment than new construction.

Installing solar panels is an effective way to make a building more sustainable and reduce fossil fuel use. The panels collect energy from the sun and convert it into electricity used in the building. The amount of energy required to power the building will determine the types and sizes of solar panels needed. A building that has more sun exposure on its roof will be more efficient at generating electricity.

Several other technologies can reduce energy usage in a building. Adding insulation keeps a building cooler in the summer and warmer in the winter, decreasing the use of heating and cooling systems. Weather-stripping windows and caulking cracks around doors and windows prevents air from escaping or entering a building. This helps to lower the cost for heating and cooling. Replacing old appliances with newer energy-efficient models can also save on energy use over time. Automated lighting, programmable thermostats, and automation systems reduce energy use by setting schedules and timers to automatically turn off lights and appliances and turn down heating and cooling systems when parts of the building are not in use.

Using natural light instead of artificial light is another way to reduce energy use. Skylights bring more natural light into the building. Painting walls and ceilings in lighter colors reflects more light, which helps to brighten up rooms. Other strategies include using window coverings that allow light to enter and removing obstructions blocking natural light.

GREEN AND COOL ROOFS

Green roofs are a layer of plants grown on a rooftop to provide shade and reduce temperatures on the roof's surface and the air around it. A green roof's temperature can be 30 to 40 degrees Fahrenheit (17–22°C) lower than that of a traditional roof.[1] This helps to lower energy used for cooling. These roofs also act as a layer of insulation, reducing the energy needed for heating. Plus, the plants on green roofs absorb carbon dioxide from the air.

Green roofs can be installed on anything from residential homes to commercial buildings. Although there are some variations in green roofs, most have similar components. A green roof includes several barriers to prevent water or plant roots from damaging the building roof. It also has a drainage layer to drain water from the roof. A layer of rich soil and green plants are on the top.

Cool roofs are another way to reduce a building's energy use. They are made of reflective materials that transfer less heat from the sun to the building than traditional roofs. This allows the building to stay cooler during hotter temperatures. As a result, the buildings with cool roofs use less energy for air-conditioning and have more comfortable inside temperatures than traditional buildings. Cool roofs are cheaper to install than green roofs. However, green roofs usually last longer because the layer of plants protects roofing materials from harsh ultraviolet radiation and extreme temperatures.

Some green roofs on residential buildings may be used for growing herbs and vegetables or as a public garden.

DISTRICT HEATING

District heating provides a promising sustainable alternative to fossil fuel–powered heating systems in buildings. It uses a network of insulated pipes to deliver hot water or steam from a central location to multiple homes or buildings. The heat can be generated from

different sources, including solar energy, geothermal sources, heat pumps powered by electricity, or fuel cells.

The district heating network carries hot supply water or steam into each building. A device called a heat exchanger transfers this heat to the building's heating network. This produces hot water for direct use and can also be used to heat rooms. After transferring its heat, the district heating supply water returns to the district heating plant where it is reheated. The water constantly circulates in closed pipelines.

SUSTAINABLE SKYSCRAPER

The Bank of America Tower in New York City is one of the world's most sustainable skyscrapers. It has several features to help reduce energy use and greenhouse gas emissions. A wind turbine on the tower's northern side captures airflow and generates electricity to supply some power to the building. The building also has photovoltaics above the entrance, which create electricity from sunlight reflected off the building's facades.

The tower relies on a cogeneration plant for more than
two-thirds of its energy.[3] A cogeneration plant produces both
electrical and thermal energy. It captures and uses heat produced
during electricity generation that would otherwise be wasted.

Cogeneration reduces the overall fuel needed by turning thermal heat into usable energy.

Inside the tower, smart controllers manage air-conditioning units to operate only when needed, which reduces unnecessary energy use. The building also uses geothermal heat from groundwater in bedrock that naturally stays around 54 degrees Fahrenheit (12°C).[4] In the winter, heat is drawn from the groundwater and circulated throughout the building.

During the summer, excess heat transfers

to the circulating water in the geothermal system to cool the
building. The building also has floor-to-ceiling insulating glass
to retain heat and let in natural light. And an automatic daylight
dimming system adjusts the
building's artificial lighting
based on the amount of
natural light available.

In addition, the Bank
of America Tower has a
green roof with a rainwater
collection system. The
rainwater is piped to a
collection tank in the
basement, where it is filtered
and treated. Then it is used
to flush the building's toilets. The building's filtration system
reduces the amount of water going into city sewers.

LIVING A SUSTAINABLE LIFE

Actor Ed Begley Jr. embraces sustainable living. When he bought
his first home in Studio City in Los Angeles, he made changes
to make it more energy efficient. "I insulated the attic and walls
and instantly saw lower gas and electric bills. Then I replaced the
light bulbs and the thermostat. Each time I saw more savings.
When I got solar, my hot water and electric bills plummeted,"
said Begley.[5]

When his family needed more space, Begley purchased another home in Studio City. He hired an architect and a contractor to make the home as energy efficient as possible. Due to its design, the construction team had to completely take apart the house. The house's doors, windows, appliances, and fixtures were donated to the charity Habitat for Humanity. Bricks and lumber were used to rebuild a church in Mexico. Approximately 96 percent of the building's original materials were recycled or salvaged.[6]

In 2016, the Begley family moved in to their new home. The house is positioned to collect heat from sunlight streaming through south-facing windows and retain the heat in heat-storing materials. The house is also divided into four zones, so the family can heat or cool the zone they're in instead of the entire home. Dimmers, sensors, and timers eliminate unnecessary energy use.

The shell of the house is made of recycled steel instead of wood. The steel frame reduces the number of trees needed for construction and is more energy efficient. Even when the outer steel layers heat up, the inner ones remain cool and help maintain stable interior temperatures.

A 10,000-gallon (38,000 L) rainwater storage tank irrigates the entire property.[7] Solar panels and two Tesla Powerwall batteries generate and store enough electricity to almost entirely power the house as well as three electric cars. A solar heating system provides hot water. Wastewater from showers and laundry is recycled and used to irrigate fruit trees on the property. Low-flow

The Begley family filmed the construction of their home for their web series, *On Begley Street*, to teach people more about sustainable living.

bathroom and kitchen fixtures reduce water consumption. For their efforts, the Begley home was awarded a platinum certification from the Leadership in Energy and Environmental Design (LEED) rating system. LEED certification is recognized worldwide as a symbol of sustainability.

The Apex Regional Landfill near Las Vegas, Nevada, is the largest landfill in the world. It covers about 2,200 acres (890 ha) of land.

CHAPTER 7

REDUCING WASTE

The increase in greenhouse gases in Earth's atmosphere is driving the planet's increasing temperatures and climate change. Solid waste is part of the problem. As solid waste decays in landfills, it releases methane. In addition, facilities that burn solid waste release nitrous oxide. Both methane and nitrous oxide are big contributors of global warming and are many times more effective at trapping heat than carbon dioxide. Therefore, reducing solid waste worldwide is one way in which climate change can be slowed.

DUMPED IN A LANDFILL

Waste is a massive problem worldwide. The amount of waste generated annually is staggering. About 2.1 billion short tons (1.9 billion metric tons) of waste is produced worldwide each year. By 2050, global waste is expected to grow to 3.4 billion short tons (3.1 billion metric tons).[1]

Waste typically includes things such as electronic devices, hazardous materials, unused food, plastic, paper, textiles, metal, and wood. Most waste ends up dumped in landfills. In the past, landfills were simply large open areas for dumping. They occupy a lot of space, often in areas with very little land resources. Traditional landfills cause significant environmental

damage. As waste decomposes, it releases methane into the atmosphere. Decomposing waste also leaks toxic chemicals and gases, contaminating nearby soil, groundwater, and air.

Some landfills have changed to become more environmentally friendly. Sanitary landfills separate waste in a system of layers that allow it to decompose safely. When the decomposing waste produces methane, sanitary landfills collect it and keep it out of the atmosphere.

RECYCLING WASTE

Instead of being dumped in a landfill, most waste can be recycled. Recycling is a process that converts waste into new, usable products. This process both decreases waste and reduces the need for new raw materials. Common recycled materials include glass, paper, metal, plastic, textiles, and electronics. To be recycled, these waste products go to a collection center where they are sorted and cleaned, and then they are processed so they can be turned into new materials.

The EPA estimates about 75 percent of waste in the United States can be recycled. However, only about 30 percent actually is recycled. The rest goes into landfills. Globally, about 91 percent of plastic is not being recycled.[3]

Waste can even be used to produce electricity. For example, in 2019, the United States used 25 million short tons (23 million metric tons) of everyday garbage and burned it to create enough electricity to power more than one million homes for an entire year.[4] However, burning waste emits harmful greenhouse gases into the atmosphere, including nitrogen oxides and carbon dioxide.

BENEFITS OF RECYCLING

Recycling reduces waste and benefits the climate. The more things are recycled, the less waste goes to landfills. In this way, recycling reduces the greenhouse gases and pollutants released into the surrounding land and the atmosphere. In many cases, it also takes less energy to make a product from recycled materials than it does to make a new product. When less energy is used to make something, fewer greenhouse gases are released into the atmosphere.

If average recycling habits increased by 82 percent by 2050, it could reduce carbon dioxide emissions by about 12.5 billion short tons (11.3 metric tons).[5] That amount of carbon dioxide is the equivalent of taking more than one billion fossil fuel–burning cars off the road for a year.[6] This data illustrates that something as simple as recycling could significantly reduce greenhouse gas emissions and slow climate change.

REDUCING PLASTIC POLLUTION

Shilpi Chhotray is an activist working with Break Free From Plastic, a global movement to reduce plastic pollution and eliminate single-use plastics. Plastic pollution continues to be a growing problem. This is because more disposable plastic items are being manufactured worldwide. "Plastics never biodegrade. They're in the environment forever. Only 9 percent of plastic waste

has actually been recycled since the 1950s—let that sink in,"
Chhotray said.[7]

To reduce plastic pollution, Chhotray and Break Free
From Plastic have started an initiative to identify the branded
packaging washing up on beaches. They rolled out a tool kit that
lists ten steps to identify and categorize the packaging waste
found during cleanups of beaches, rivers, lakes, and watersheds.
"If we can get data on the number of packaged items we find, we
can say to companies, 'Hey, this is your waste, and you need to be
responsible for it.' Through corporate campaigning, we can hold
industries accountable," said Chhotray.[8] Since the first event in
2017, more than 2,300 events in 87 countries have collected and
categorized more than 2.1 million pieces of plastic waste.[9]

The efforts of Break Free From Plastic

and other activists and organizations have influenced how people produce, use, and recycle plastics. Some communities have passed bans on single-use plastics. Others have created zero-waste communities and plastic-free schools. For example, Alex Gordon, who was a student at Eckerd College in Florida, collected data on plastic pollution for three years. She then took the results to her school administrators. In 2019, Gordon persuaded the school to sign a pledge to become a plastic-free campus.

Identifying the makers of plastic pollution has also had an effect on holding plastic producers accountable for plastic waste. In one town in India, a three-week analysis of 75 households identified the top plastic-polluting brands. With the data, local officials demanded that responsible corporations find ways to reduce plastic packaging and pollution.

COMPOSTING FOOD WASTE

Food is the largest source of waste in landfills, according to the US Food and Drug Administration (FDA). Experts estimate that food waste makes up about 24 percent of garbage.[10] Composting, a way to recycle food waste and other organic

material, is one way to reduce food waste in landfills. It also helps to lower greenhouse gas emissions related to food waste. Pashon Murray, cofounder of the composting organization Detroit Dirt

What Is Composting?

Composting is a way to recycle food waste and other organic matter. This process accelerates decomposition by providing a favorable environment for bacteria, worms, fungi, and other organisms to break down the organic material. The decomposed matter is called compost and is rich in nutrients. Compost can be reused as fertile soil for gardening and agriculture. Composting removes food waste from landfills and turns it into something that can be reused.

in Michigan, is working to reduce food waste across the United States. Murray created a closed-loop composting system, which is a system where waste is continuously reused by gardening and composting it.

Murray's interest in combating food waste began at a young age. As a kid, she rode with her father to landfills for his small Michigan contracting business. She also visited her grandparents' farm in Mississippi. With this knowledge, Murray began composting with the urban farming movement in Detroit.

Today, Murray and Detroit Dirt have partnered with corporations such as General Motors and Blue Cross Blue Shield to pick up their food waste and with local breweries for their spent grain, which is the by-product of used grain. Detroit Dirt has even partnered with the Detroit Zoo to pick up manure from herbivores. Instead of these wastes going into a landfill, Detroit Dirt uses them to create rich compost for the city's gardeners and farmers. "By composting and keeping waste out of landfills, we're solving a climate issue because food waste contributes to global warming," Murray said.[12]

TURNING PLASTIC WASTE INTO BRICKS

Recycling plastic reduces greenhouse gas emissions in two main ways. First, it reduces the amount of waste in landfills and the related methane emissions. It also reduces the need to manufacture new products and materials, which reduces the associated greenhouse gas emissions.

In Kenya, engineer Nzambi Matee has found a creative way to recycle plastic waste. She created a new way to convert plastic waste into sustainable materials. Matee is the founder of Gjenge Makers, a start-up company that uses recycled plastic and sand to make bricks that are stronger than concrete. She was inspired to start her company after regularly finding plastic bags discarded along the streets of Nairobi, Kenya's capital city.

Matee, who has a background in material science and worked as an oil industry engineer, set up a small lab in her mother's backyard. She began to create and test bricks made from plastic and sand. Through trial and error, Matee

Plastic Waste Becomes Art

Some artists are taking plastic waste and transforming it into works of art. Israeli artist Beverly Barkat has collected plastic trash for years, including bags, bottles, cartons, cups, lids, and wrappers. She turned the plastic waste into *Earth Poetica*, a 13-foot (4 m) globe sculpture.[13] The globe was displayed in New York City for World Environment Day in 2023. Barkat shaped pieces of plastic waste in clear epoxy resin to make the globe's spherical shape. She hopes the work will bring awareness and action to the problem of plastic pollution worldwide.

discovered that some plastics bind better than others. It took her about a year to find the proper ratios of sand to plastics to create the bricks. She also designed the machines needed to manufacture the bricks.

Today, Matee's company gathers plastic waste from packaging factories or other recyclers. A machine mixes the plastic waste with sand at very high temperatures. A second machine compresses the mixture into a brick form. The company produces about 500 to 1,000 bricks daily, which recycles nearly 1,100 pounds (500 kg) of plastic waste.[14] The recycled bricks are very durable and cost less to maintain than traditional pavers. They are used in houses, schools, and streets. Matee said:

> Plastic waste is not just a Kenya problem, but it's a worldwide problem. . . . Here in Nairobi, we generate about 500 metric tonnes [550 short tons] of plastic waste every single day and only a fraction of that is recycled. We decided what more can we do instead of just sitting in the sidelines and complaining. Essentially, companies have to pay to dispose the waste, so we solved their problem. That waste essentially comes for free.[15]

In 2020, the UN named Nzambi Matee a Young Champion of the Earth. The award provides funding for individuals who are finding new ways to help the environment.

Many forests around the world, including the Amazon rainforest, are threatened due to deforestation.

RESTORING AND PROTECTING NATURE

Trees, plants, soil, and oceans have a unique role in the battle against climate change. They are carbon sinks, which means they absorb more carbon dioxide from the atmosphere than they release. Without Earth's natural carbon sinks, levels of greenhouse gases would rise significantly, heating the planet and making life on Earth impossible.

NATURE'S CARBON STORAGE

Healthy ecosystems absorb and store massive amounts of carbon dioxide from the atmosphere. Wetlands and mangrove forests in coastal regions collect and store carbon in the roots of trees and plants. Freshwater wetlands store carbon in the soil and in the roots of plants. In forests, trees and other plants take in carbon dioxide for photosynthesis and store carbon in their trunks, absorbing approximately 30 percent of global carbon dioxide emissions annually.[1] The world's oceans also absorb and store significant amounts of carbon dioxide and capture heat radiated by greenhouse gases in the atmosphere.

Yet Earth's forests, ecosystems, soil, and oceans are increasingly threatened. Forests cover one-third of Earth's land. They provide habitats for many species of plants and animals. And they are one of the planet's hardest-working carbon sinks.

However, humans have repeatedly cleared forests to make way for shopping malls, neighborhoods, and other developments. They cut down trees to use as lumber, paper, and other products. Between 1990 and 2015, the number of forests being cleared per hour was equal to the size of 1,000 football fields, according to the World Bank. "It makes no sense to clearcut one of the world's most important tools for fighting climate change," said Anthony Swift, director of the Natural Resources Defense Council's Canada Project.[2]

Earth's soil absorbs about 25 percent of human-generated carbon emissions annually.[3] Much of the carbon is stored in peatland or permafrost. However, increasing demand for food production, chemical pollution, and climate change are destroying these areas.

Since humans began burning fossil fuels for energy, the world's oceans have absorbed about 25 percent of the resulting carbon dioxide emissions.[4] In the ocean, microscopic marine algae and organisms called phytoplankton absorb carbon dioxide. But plastic pollution in oceans is disrupting that process. Plastic gets into the ocean in various ways, such as littering and illegal dumping. Over time, larger plastic objects break down into particles called microplastics. Microplastics are less than 0.2 inches (0.5 cm) in size, yet they make up 90 percent of the ocean's plastic pollution.[6] Microplastics disrupt the ocean's ability to absorb carbon by affecting phytoplankton. When phytoplankton eat microplastics, it slows the rate at which they trap carbon in the ocean, so less carbon is absorbed overall.

ADDING CARBON

Clearing forests and wetlands does more than remove carbon sinks. It also increases carbon emissions. As a tree dies, the carbon it has stored over its lifetime is released. That carbon dioxide can then be absorbed by nearby young trees growing in the forest.

However, when a forest is cut down or burned, the trees release all the carbon they have absorbed. When the land is cleared for development, there are no trees left to absorb the released carbon and no plans to allow new trees to regrow. If the land is used as farmland or becomes grassland, the smaller plants absorb some carbon, but not as much as the larger, mature trees. The carbon that cannot be absorbed stays in the atmosphere, increasing the greenhouse effect.

RESTORING NATURE

Human activity has increased the amount of greenhouse gases in the atmosphere while also limiting the ability of natural systems to absorb and store carbon. To address the problem, some activists and communities have launched efforts to restore natural habitats. This includes restoring wetlands, forests, and other ecosystems.

The Dutch Slough Tidal Marsh Restoration Project in northern California is an ongoing tidal wetlands restoration effort in the Sacramento–San Joaquin Delta region. Beginning in 2018, the California Department of Water Resources started repairing the land and planted thousands of plants, shrubs, and trees. The next step was to allow water from the delta channels to move in and out of the area with daily tides. The project reestablished the area's tidal marsh and became an essential habitat for local fish and wildlife.

The Dutch Slough project has also become an important part in the battle against climate change. Wetlands are an essential natural carbon sink. All wetlands store carbon from the atmosphere in living vegetation and in their organic soils and sediments that build up over the years. Although plant material releases carbon when it decomposes, the process is much slower in wetlands because the plants are underwater without oxygen. As a result, the plant material remains intact in the wetland soil, and the carbon is not released into the atmosphere.

The project's restoration efforts are paying off. Biometeorology professor Dennis Baldocchi and his team at the University of California in Berkeley measured greenhouse gases and other data in the marsh. After more than a year of collecting data, Baldocchi said the data showed the restored Dutch Slough is a powerful carbon sink. It absorbs carbon dioxide and stores it in the ground instead of releasing it into the atmosphere, where it would contribute to climate change.

RESTORING FORESTS

Other climate efforts are focused on protecting and restoring the world's forests. Txai Suruí is a climate activist in Rondônia, Brazil. There, she has seen how climate change is already harming the Amazon rainforest. Located in northern Brazil, Rondônia has been greatly affected by deforestation. For decades, deforestation has been widespread in the region. Forests have been cleared for many uses, including farms, ranches, roads, mining, and logging. As a result, biodiversity in the region has been reduced, and rivers are running dry.

To bring attention to the problem of deforestation, Suruí founded the Indigenous Youth Movement of Rondônia. Her work focuses on climate justice and preserving the rights and

ELIZABETH WATHUTI

Elizabeth Wathuti is an environmental and climate activist. Growing up in Kenya, Wathuti witnessed the devastation of deforestation in the country's central highlands. The forests where she played as a child were cut down, and the streams where she drank were dried up or polluted. These changes left Wathuti angry and upset. They also inspired her to take action to fight deforestation and climate change.

In 2016, Wathuti founded the Green Generation Initiative, an organization that helps local communities carry out nature-based solutions to slow climate change. The organization also works to encourage and educate youth and communities to become environmentally conscious.

Wathuti spoke at the UN Climate Change Conference (COP26) in 2021. She shared stories of how Kenyans are experiencing climate change. She also urged the audience to focus on action to face the global challenge of climate change.

In 2019, Elizabeth Wathuti received the Diana Award, which honors young people making positive changes to the world.

land of Indigenous tribes in Brazil. She has campaigned against deforestation in Brazil and worldwide.

In 2021, 24-year-old Suruí spoke at the UN Climate Change Conference (COP26) in Glasgow, Scotland. In her address, she discussed the urgent need to stop the expansion of fossil fuel use and end deforestation. Suruí said, "Today, the climate is warming. The animals are disappearing. The rivers are dying, and our plants don't flower like they did before. . . . The Earth is speaking. She tells us that we have no more time!"[8]

> "Today . . . it is becoming harder and harder to reverse forest loss and land degradation. It is time to prioritize people and our planet over short-term profits.[9]
>
> —Elizabeth Wathuti, environmental and climate activist, 2023

PROTECTING OCEANS

Earth's oceans are essential to slowing climate change. However, increasing amounts of greenhouse gases in the atmosphere have affected the ocean's health. Warming waters and increasing acidity have harmed the ocean's ecosystems and organisms. These changes have also reduced the ocean's ability to absorb carbon dioxide. "The Ocean must play a critical role in helping the world counter the climate crisis," said Leticia Carvalho, head of the Marine and Freshwater Branch of the UN Environment Programme (UNEP). "But right now, many marine environments, including coastal ecosystems, are under threat . . . We have no choice but to dramatically scale up action and funding to protect them."[10]

The ocean's ability to absorb carbon relies on its rich biodiversity. Mangrove forests in salty coastal waters store up to four times more carbon than tropical forests.[11] Seagrass sediment is one of the world's most efficient carbon stores. Even the bodies of marine animals store carbon. However, human activity, pollution, and warming waters are negatively affecting the ocean's health and its ecosystems.

Several initiatives are underway to protect the world's oceans. One project is happening in Gazi Bay, Kenya. More than 3,000 residents in the community have stopped logging mangroves. Instead, the residents are replanting mangroves to restore the vital resource. A community-led project called Mikoko Pamoja, which means "mangroves together" in Swahili, pays residents to grow mangroves instead of cutting them down. International companies pay to restore mangrove forests as a way to offset the greenhouse gas emissions they generate in their business operations worldwide. Under the project, more than 5,000 mangrove seedlings have already been planted in Gazi Bay.[12]

The Nature Conservancy and the Virginia Institute of Marine Science have teamed up for an extensive seagrass meadow restoration project in Virginia. Researchers and volunteers have planted more than 70 million eelgrass seeds across a 494-acre (200-ha) area near the southern end of Virginia's Eastern Shore region.[13] Planting the seeds sparked the natural spread of eelgrass across the region.

Along with restoring mangrove forests, the Mikoko Pamoja project has provided more income and education to the local villagers in Gazi Bay.

The project has created more than 8,900 acres (3,600 ha) of new seagrass beds that act as a carbon sink. When measurements were taken in 2020, they showed that these seagrass beds store about 3,300 short tons (3,000 metric tons) of carbon and more than 660 short tons (600 metric tons) of nitrogen annually. Marine ecologist Carlos Duarte said, "It's an exemplar of how nature-based solutions can help mitigate climate change."[14]

Climate activists will often take action by going to protests or speaking about solutions to combat climate change.

CHAPTER 9

GET INVOLVED IN SOLUTIONS

Every day, more people, organizations, businesses, and governments are becoming engaged in protecting the planet. People worldwide are coming together to take action against the effects of climate change. By working together, people can protect the planet and help ensure all living things continue to live and thrive on Earth.

MITIGATING CLIMATE CHANGE

Climate change is a global issue. But there are steps individuals can take to help mitigate the effects of climate change. While it may not seem as though individual actions will solve the problem, over time, any action to reduce global emissions, whether big or small, can add up and make a difference. These steps can be as simple as making daily changes to reduce greenhouse gas emissions and support climate solutions. People can use more energy-efficient appliances, reduce their plastic use, waste less food, walk and bike instead of drive, turn off electronics that are not in use, and more.

There are also many ways for individuals and groups to get involved on a larger scale. People can volunteer to do things such as planting trees at a public park or picking up trash on a beach. In addition, they can speak up to businesses and government officials about climate change issues.

If a business is using products that contribute to large amounts of greenhouse gas emissions, people can contact those businesses to get them to use more renewable sources instead. Contacting government officials, whether local, state, or federal, is a great way to work toward new laws and regulations that reduce carbon emissions. Every person around the world can take action to help solve the global threat of climate change.

ENERGY ACTIONS

Today, most energy still comes from fossil fuel sources. Electricity and heat are often produced by burning coal, oil, and natural gas. Reducing energy use at home reduces the amount of fossil fuels burned and in turn reduces greenhouse gas emissions.

Most people can make a few simple changes at home to reduce energy use. They can switch to LED light bulbs and install energy-efficient appliances. Washing clothes in cold water instead of hot water also uses less energy. Installing better insulation can help reduce the need for heating and air-conditioning. Some homeowners choose to replace an existing oil or gas furnace with an electric heat pump to lower their emissions even more.

Another way to reduce emissions is to switch from fossil fuel energy sources to renewable energy sources at home. Solar panels generate power for appliances, heating, and cooling. Small residential wind turbines provide usable electrical energy to individual homes. Switching from energy produced by fossil fuels to renewable energy at home can reduce a person's carbon emissions by up to 1.5 short tons (1.4 metric tons) per year.[1]

TRANSPORTATION ACTIONS

Fossil fuel–powered vehicles are a significant source of greenhouse gas emissions. One way to lower emissions is for people to walk or ride bikes instead of driving. For longer trips, people can carpool or take a train or bus to reduce the number of vehicles on the road. Not using a car can decrease a person's carbon emissions by up to two short tons (1.8 metric tons) every year.[2]

Driving an electric vehicle instead of a gasoline-powered one is also an environmentally friendly choice. Every year, automakers offer more affordable electric car models. Electric cars reduce air pollution and produce significantly less emissions than gas- or diesel-powered vehicles. Although electric cars are not entirely emission-free as they may be powered by electricity produced from fossil fuels, they are still a lower-emission option than traditional cars.

Airplanes produce a large amount of greenhouse gas emissions. Another way for people to make a difference is by taking fewer flights. People may be able to travel by train instead. With advances in virtual technology, an in-person meeting might not even be necessary. Instead, the meeting could take place virtually.

CREATE LESS WASTE

Many goods and products people use daily, such as clothing, electronics, and plastics, use fossil fuels at many points in the production process. The extracting of raw materials, manufacturing of products, and transporting of finished goods all use fossil fuel energy and generate greenhouse gas emissions. Fewer new goods are needed when people buy fewer products, helping reduce emissions at every point in the production process. Instead of buying new, people can shop garage sales or secondhand stores, reuse and repurpose existing items, and buy fewer goods overall.

Recycling goods from metals and clothing to plastics and paper reduces the need for new products and generates

less waste. Every 2.2 pounds (1 kg) of new textiles produced creates about 37 pounds (17 kg) of carbon emissions.[4] Therefore, something as simple as buying a used shirt instead of shopping for a new one is a simple way to take action and reduce waste.

Reducing food waste can also lower greenhouse gas emissions. Food waste in landfills can emit large amounts of methane as it decomposes. To reduce food waste, people should try to buy only the food they need, use what they buy, and compost anything unused. Reducing food waste can lower a person's carbon emissions by about 660 pounds (300 kg) annually.[6]

ONE FAMILY'S EFFORTS

Andrea Loewen Nair, her husband, and her two sons have made several changes to their lives to live more sustainably and reduce their emissions. One of the biggest changes was where they lived in the city of London in Ontario, Canada. The family moved from the suburbs to downtown where they could be closer to work and school. The family now walks and bikes almost everywhere they need to go. Andrea uses a bike for most of her daily transportation and errands. The family has one car they use occasionally to drive longer distances. "We can get to 90 percent of where we need to go by just walking 15 minutes," said Andrea.[7]

The family also made changes by renovating

their 1920s home to make it more energy efficient. They installed new windows and foam insulation. In addition, they replaced the heating and cooling systems with newer, more efficient systems that use less energy. These changes have significantly reduced the family's natural gas use at home.

The family is already planning more changes for the future. They hope to install solar panels to provide electricity. They also plan to replace their car with an electric vehicle and install electric vehicle charging equipment in their garage. The family aims to live as close to net-zero as possible. Andrea said, "We're making this commitment to our children and their children to do better, so we're doing as much as we can, and I like how that feels."[8]

CLIMATE CHANGE AFFECTS ALL

Climate change affects every living thing on Earth. From extreme weather events to rising sea levels, there is no doubt that climate change is here. As the impacts of climate change

Planting trees and recycling properly are just some of the many ways people can get involved with fighting climate change.

grow more intense, more people are speaking out and working toward solutions. By spreading awareness about the issue of climate change, people motivate others to take action for a cleaner and cooler world.

Climate activism can sometimes be small and simple, such as turning off all electronics that are not in use. Other times, larger events, such as protests, can help spread awareness and inspire more people to make changes to protect Earth and its climate. Worldwide, more people, organizations, businesses, and governments are joining the battle against climate change. When people come together to find solutions for Earth's changing climate, big and small actions alike can add up to make the world a better place to live.

> When enough people come together, then change will come and we can achieve almost anything. So instead of looking for hope—start creating it.[9]
>
> —Greta Thunberg, climate activist, 2021

CLIMATE CHANGE PROBLEMS

- Human activity, mainly the burning of fossil fuels, has caused more greenhouse gases to be released into Earth's atmosphere, which is driving Earth's warming trend and current climate changes.

- Greenhouse gases, such as carbon dioxide, trap heat in the atmosphere and radiate it back to Earth's surface.

- Deforestation and damage to wetlands and oceans have reduced Earth's natural ability to absorb carbon from the atmosphere.

- Earth's warming climate has caused hotter temperatures, more frequent extreme weather events, rising sea levels, melting of polar and glacier ice, and changing habitats for animals and plants.

- People burn fossil fuels such as coal, oil, and natural gas to heat and cool buildings, run factories, generate electricity, and fuel vehicles.

CLIMATE CHANGE SOLUTIONS

- Replacing fossil fuels with renewable energy sources such as wind and solar power can reduce greenhouse gas emissions.

- Driving electric vehicles, taking public transportation, walking, and biking can lower emissions of greenhouse gases and pollution.

- Using energy-efficient technologies, such as green roofs, automated lighting, and improved insulation, can reduce energy needs in buildings.

- Recycling and reducing waste decreases the level of harmful emissions from waste in landfills and can reduce the use of energy and resources to produce new items.

- Protecting and restoring nature's carbon sinks, such as forests, oceans, and wetlands, can improve the planet's ability to absorb excess carbon from the atmosphere and slow climate change.

- Reduce energy use by turning off appliances and lights when not in use and switching to energy-efficient appliances.

- Buy fewer new items and recycle more to reduce waste.

- Volunteer to plant trees or clean up garbage.

- Contact government officials about creating laws that will help fight climate change.

QUOTE

"We're the first generation to see the effects of climate change, and the last generation who can do anything about it."

—*Michael McGinn, former mayor of Seattle, Washington, 2013*

algae
Plantlike organisms that mostly grow in water and are often green, blue, red, or brown colored.

biodiversity
The many different plants and animals in an ecosystem.

deforestation
The action of clearing a large group of trees.

emission
The production and discharge of something such as smoke, gas, or chemicals into the air.

glacier
A large, thickened mass of ice formed from fallen snow that has compacted and been added to over many years.

groundwater
Water that is naturally stored underground in caverns, cavities, and soil.

habitat
The natural environment of an organism.

mangrove
A shrub or tree with tangled roots that grows near the coast in tropical swamps that flood at high tide.

marsh
A type of low-lying wetland that can be tidal or nontidal and that is flooded during high tide or wet seasons; most marshes are waterlogged all the time.

mitigate
To reduce or prevent something, such as greenhouse gas emissions.

photosynthesis
The process used by plants and other organisms to convert sunlight into usable energy.

pollutant
A substance that is harmful to the environment.

precipitation
Moisture that falls from the atmosphere in the form of rain, sleet, snow, or hail.

radiate
To spread outward.

reservoir
A human-made lake for storing water for people to use.

sediment
Tiny fragments of rock and other particles that settle to the bottom of a body of water.

sustainable
A practice that avoids depleting natural resources.

turbine
A machine that uses a fast-moving flow of water, steam, gas, air, or other fluid to produce energy.

wetland
An area where the land is saturated with water.

SELECTED BIBLIOGRAPHY

"Climate Action." *United Nations*, n.d., un.org. Accessed 10 Aug. 2023.

Green, Amy. "Meet the Teenager Who Helped Push Florida toward Cleaner Energy." *NPR*, 14 Aug. 2022, npr.org. Accessed 11 Aug. 2023.

Turrentine, Jeff. "What Are the Solutions to Climate Change?" *Natural Resources Defense Council*, 13 Dec. 2022, nrdc.org. Accessed 9 Aug. 2023.

FURTHER READINGS

Buckey, A. W. *Pollution*. Abdo, 2025.

Sarah, Rachel. *Girl Warriors: How 25 Young Activists Are Saving the Earth*. Chicago Review Press, 2021.

Woodward, John. *Climate Change*. DK, 2021.

ONLINE RESOURCES

To learn more about climate change, please visit **abdobooklinks.com** or scan this QR code. These links are routinely monitored and updated to provide the most current information available.

MORE INFORMATION

For more information on this subject, contact or visit the
following organizations:

Environmental Defense Fund
257 Park Ave. S., 17th Floor
New York, NY 10010
edf.org
The Environmental Defense Fund is an environmental advocacy group
that focuses on global warming, ecosystem restoration, oceans, and
human health.

Greenpeace
1300 Eye St. NW, Ste. 1100 East
Washington, DC 20005
greenpeace.org
Greenpeace is a global network of organizations working to bring
awareness and promote solutions to environmental problems,
including climate change.

The Nature Conservancy
4245 North Fairfax Dr., Ste. 100
Arlington, VA 22203
nature.org
The Nature Conservancy is a global environmental nonprofit working
to provide education and promote solutions to climate change and
biodiversity loss.

CHAPTER 1. FLOODWATERS RISING

1. Sue Halpern. "Vermont's Catastrophic Floods and the Spread of Unnatural Disasters." *New Yorker*, 12 July 2023, newyorker.com. Accessed 29 Nov. 2023.

2. Anna Betts. "What to Know about Vermont's Devastating Floods." *New York Times*, 12 July 2023, nytimes.com. Accessed 29 Nov. 2023.

3. Joel Banner Baird. "Looking Back 10 Years at the Devastation Wrought by Tropical Storm Irene in Vermont." *Burlington Free Press*, 27 Aug. 2021, burlingtonfreepress.com. Accessed 29 Nov. 2023.

CHAPTER 2. THE SCIENCE OF CLIMATE CHANGE

1. "2023 Shatters Climate Records, with Major Impacts." *World Meteorological Organization*, 30 Nov. 2023, wmo.int. Accessed 27 Dec. 2023.

2. Alejandra Borunda. "Why Are Our Oceans Getting Warmer?" *National Geographic*, 1 May 2023, nationalgeographic.com. Accessed 29 Nov. 2023.

3. Rebecca Lindsey and Luann Dahlman. "Climate Change: Global Temperature." *Climate.gov*, 18 Jan. 2023, climate.gov. Accessed 29 Nov. 2023.

4. "How Do We Know Climate Change Is Real?" *National Aeronautics and Space Administration*, n.d., climate.nasa.gov. Accessed 11 Jan. 2024.

5. "Sources of Greenhouse Gas Emissions." *Environmental Protection Agency*, n.d., epa.gov. Accessed 29 Nov. 2023.

6. Holli Riebeek. "Global Warming." *Earth Observatory*, 2 June 2010, earthobservatory.nasa.gov. Accessed 29 Nov. 2023.

7. Riebeek, "Global Warming."

8. "2023 Shatters Climate Records."

9. Michael Patrick McGinn. "Let's Prevent This Crisis: A Letter to Harvard's President Faust." *HuffPost*, 17 Oct. 2013, huffpost.com. Accessed 29 Nov. 2023.

10. Josie Garthwaite. "Earth Likely to Cross Critical Climate Thresholds Even If Emissions Decline, Stanford Study Finds." *Stanford University*, 20 Jan. 2023. Accessed 29 Nov. 2023.

11. Betsy Reed. "'Our House Is on Fire': Greta Thunberg, 16, Urges Leaders to Act on Climate." *Guardian*, 25 Jan. 2019, theguardian.com. Accessed 29 Nov. 2023.

CHAPTER 3. THE HISTORY OF CLIMATE CHANGE

1. Amara Huddleston. "Happy 200th Birthday to Eunice Foote, Hidden Climate Science Pioneer." *Climate.gov*, 17 July 2019, climate.gov. Accessed 29 Nov. 2023.

2. Clive Thompson. "How 19th Century Scientists Predicted Global Warming." *JSTOR Daily*, 17 Dec. 2019, daily.jstor.org. Accessed 29 Nov. 2023.

3. Thompson, "How 19th Century Scientists Predicted Global Warming."

4. Thompson, "How 19th Century Scientists Predicted Global Warming."

5. "A Brief History of Climate Change Discoveries." *UK Research and Innovation*, n.d., discover.ukri.org. Accessed 29 Nov. 2023.

6. "A Brief History of Climate Change Discoveries."

7. Rebecca Lindsey. "Climate Change: Mountain Glaciers." *Climate.gov*, 14 Feb. 2020, climate.gov. Accessed 29 Nov. 2023.

8. Lindsay Maizland. "Global Climate Agreements: Successes and Failures." *Council on Foreign Relations*, 15 Sept. 2023, cfr.org. Accessed 29 Nov. 2023.

9. António Guterres. "Remarks at 2019 Climate Action Summit." *United Nations*, 23 Sept. 2019, un.org. Accessed 29 Nov. 2023.

10. "The Paris Agreement." *United Nations*, n.d., un.org. Accessed 29 Nov. 2023.

CHAPTER 4. REPLACING FOSSIL FUELS

1. "Causes and Effects of Climate Change." *United Nations*, n.d., un.org. Accessed 29 Nov. 2023.

2. "Electricity Explained." *US Energy Information Administration*, Feb. 2023, eia.gov. Accessed 29 Nov. 2023.

3. "Electricity Explained."

4. "What Is US Electricity Generation by Energy Source?" *US Energy Information Administration*, 26 Sept. 2023, eia.gov. Accessed 29 Nov. 2023.

5. Khalil Shahyd. "Residential Energy Efficiency Is Largest Source of CO2 Reduction Potential." *Natural Resources Defense Council*, 5 Oct. 2017, nrdc.org. Accessed 29 Nov. 2023.

6. Amy Green. "Meet the Teenager Who Helped Push Florida toward Cleaner Energy." *NPR*, 14 Aug. 2022, npr.org. Accessed 29 Nov. 2023.

7. Zoe Sayler. "Those Meddling Kids!" *Grist*, 22 July 2019, grist.org. Accessed 29 Nov. 2023.

8. Green, "Meet the Teenager Who Helped Push Florida toward Cleaner Energy."

CHAPTER 5. SUSTAINABLE TRANSPORTATION

1. "Sources of Greenhouse Gas Emissions." *Environmental Protection Agency*, n.d., epa.gov. Accessed 29 Nov. 2023.

2. "Sources of Greenhouse Gas Emissions."

3. Jackie Snow. "Greener Air Travel Will Depend on These Emerging Technologies." *National Geographic*, 15 Jan. 2021, nationalgeographic.com. Accessed 29 Nov. 2023.

4. Matt Pressman. "The Future for Electric Vehicles—A Few Analysts Weigh In." *Clean Technica*, 2018, cleantechnica.com. Accessed 30 Nov. 2023.

5. Peter Simek. "How to Fix Public Transit: A Case Study." *D*, 26 Nov. 2019, dmagazine.com. Accessed 30 Nov. 2023.

6. Nathaniel Meyersohn. "Congestion Pricing Is Coming to New York City, Officials Announce." *CNN*, 26 June 2023, cnn.com. Accessed 30 Nov. 2023.

7. Catherine Clifford. "New York Gov. Hochul Touts NYC as First U.S. City to Move Forward with Traffic Congestion Pricing." *CNBC*, 27 June 2023, cnbc.com. Accessed 30 Nov. 2023.

8. "Governor Hochul Announces First-in-Nation Congestion Pricing Will Move Forward, Improving Air Quality and Reducing Traffic." *New York State*, 27 June 2023, governor.ny.gov. Accessed 30 Nov. 2023.

9. Karen Hallisey. "How Riding a Bike Benefits the Environment." *University of California, Los Angeles*, 11 May 2022, transportation.ucla.edu. Accessed 30 Nov. 2023.

10. Maya Norris. "Chicago, Bike Grid Now! Pushes for Easy-to-Implement Bicycle Infrastructure." *Active Transportation Alliance*, 11 Feb. 2023, activetrans.org. Accessed 30 Nov. 2023.

11. Norris, "Chicago, Bike Grid Now! Pushes for Bicycle Infrastructure."

12. Heather Ervin. "Sea Change Ferry Arrives in San Francisco." *Marine Log*, 14 Mar. 2023, marinelog.com. Accessed 30 Nov. 2023.

13. Norris, "Chicago, Bike Grid Now! Pushes for Bicycle Infrastructure."

14. Norris, "Chicago, Bike Grid Now! Pushes for Bicycle Infrastructure."

CHAPTER 6. SUSTAINABLE BUILDINGS

1. "Using Green Roofs to Reduce Heat Islands." *Environmental Protection Agency*, 28 June 2023, epa.gov. Accessed 30 Nov. 2023.

2. "Top 5 Benefits of Green Building." *Inogen Alliance*, 17 Aug. 2022, inogenalliance.com. Accessed 30 Nov. 2023.

3. "Bank of America Tower—Leader in Sustainability?" *Smart CRE*, 2 Apr. 2022, smart-cre.com. Accessed 30 Nov. 2023.

4. "Bank of America Tower—Leader in Sustainability?"

5. Erica Holthausen. "Go Inside the LEED Platinum Home of Actor and Activist Ed Begley Jr." *U.S. Green Building Council*, 2018, usgbc.org. Accessed 30 Nov. 2023.

6. Holthausen, "LEED Platinum Home of Ed Begley Jr."

7. Chelsee Lowe. "Step Inside the Eco-Friendly Home of Ed Begley Jr. and Rachelle Carson-Begley." *Ventura Blvd*, n.d., ourventurablvd.com. Accessed 30 Nov. 2023.

CHAPTER 7. REDUCING WASTE

1. Elizabeth Long. "How Much Do We Waste? A Data-Driven Guide to Waste and Landfills." *Environmental Protection*, 13 July 2022, eponline.com. Accessed 30 Nov. 2023.

2. "74 Recycling Facts + Statistics for 2023." *Recycle Track Systems*, 2 Jan. 2023, rts.com. Accessed 30 Nov. 2023.

3. Long, "How Much Do We Waste?"

4. Micah Meghreblian. "Technologies That Divert Waste from Landfills." *Cleanup News*, 1 Sept. 2021, 1news.org. Accessed 30 Nov. 2023.

5. "Recycling." *Project Drawdown*, n.d., drawdown.org. Accessed 30 Nov. 2023.

6. Celeste Robinson. "Recycling and Climate Change." *University of Colorado Boulder*, 18 Mar. 2021, colorado.edu. Accessed 30 Nov. 2023.

7. Jackie Homan. "3 Environmental Activists Who Are Changing the World." *Repeller*, 20 Apr. 2018, repeller.com. Accessed 30 Nov. 2023.

8. Homan, "3 Environmental Activists."

9. "About the Brand Audit." *#BreakFreeFromPlastic*, n.d., breakfreefromplastic.org. Accessed 30 Nov. 2023.

10. "Food Loss and Waste." *US Food and Drug Administration*, n.d., fda.gov. Accessed 30 Nov. 2023.

11. "Food Loss and Waste."

12. Homan, "3 Environmental Activists."

13. James Barron. "The Art of Reusing Plastic." *New York Times*, 6 June 2023, nytimes.com. Accessed 30 Nov. 2023.

14. "Kenyan Startup Founder Nzambi Matee Recycles Plastic to Make Bricks That Are Stronger than Concrete." *World Architecture Community*, 12 Feb. 2021, worldarchitecture.org. Accessed 30 Nov. 2023.

15. "Nzambi Matee Recycles Plastic to Make Bricks."

16. "Why Reduce & Reuse?" *Addison County Solid Waste Management District*, n.d., addisoncountyrecycles.org. Accessed 30 Nov. 2023.

CHAPTER 8. RESTORING AND PROTECTING NATURE

1. Melissa Denchak. "Want to Fight Climate Change? Stop Clearcutting Our Carbon Sinks." *Natural Resources Defense Council*, 13 Dec. 2017, nrdc.org. Accessed 30 Nov. 2023.

2. Denchak, "Want to Fight Climate Change?"

3. "What Is a Carbon Sink?" *ClientEarth*, 22 Dec. 2020, clientearth.org. Accessed 30 Nov. 2023.

4. "The Ocean—The World's Greatest Ally against Climate Change." *United Nations*, n.d., un.org. Accessed 30 Nov. 2023.

5. Katie Hoover and Anne A. Riddle. "US Forest Carbon Data: In Brief." *Congressional Research Service*, 6 June 2023, congress.gov. Accessed 30 Nov. 2023.

6. "How Does Plastic Get into the Ocean?" *International Fund for Animal Welfare*, 12 July 2021, ifaw.org. Accessed 30 Nov. 2023.

7. Scott Faber and Geoff Horsfield. "Will Agriculture Be America's Leading Source of Greenhouse Gas Emissions?" *Environmental Working Group*, 28 Feb. 2023, ewg.org. Accessed 30 Nov. 2023.

8. Emily Baumgaertner, Kate Linthicum, and Parth M. N. "Young Climate Activists Warn Their Elders: Stop Destroying the Planet." *Los Angeles Times*, 4 Nov. 2021, latimes.com. Accessed 30 Nov. 2023.

9. Tess Lowery, Fadeke Banjo, and Lana Lenfant Al Zouheiri. "11 of the Most Powerful Quotes from Climate Activists at Power Our Planet: Live in Paris." *Global Citizen*, 22 June 2023, globalcitizen.org. Accessed 30 Nov. 2023.

10. "Why Protecting the Ocean and Wetlands Can Help Fight the Climate Crisis." *United Nations Environment Programme*, 11 Nov. 2022, unep.org. Accessed 30 Nov. 2023.

11. "Ocean and Wetlands Can Help Fight Climate Crisis."

12. Cece Siago. "A Kenyan Village Replants Essential Mangrove Forests." *One Earth*, 10 Nov. 2021, oneearth.org. Accessed 30 Nov. 2023.

13. Joseph Polidoro. "How Planting 70 Million Eelgrass Seeds Led to an Ecosystem's Rapid Recovery." *ScienceNews*, 14 Oct. 2020, sciencenews.org. Accessed 30 Nov. 2023.

14. Polidoro, "Planting 70 Million Eelgrass Seeds."

CHAPTER 9. GET INVOLVED IN SOLUTIONS

1. "Actions for a Healthy Planet." *United Nations*, n.d., un.org. Accessed 30 Nov. 2023.

2. "Actions for a Healthy Planet."

3. "Carbon Footprint Factsheet." *University of Michigan*, 2023, css.umich.edu. Accessed 30 Nov. 2023.

4. "Actions for a Healthy Planet."

5. Melissa Denchak. "How You Can Stop Global Warming." *Natural Resources Defense Council*, 7 Aug. 2023, nrdc.org. Accessed 30 Nov. 2023.

6. "Actions for a Healthy Planet."

7. "This London Family Ditched the Suburbs for Downtown to Lower Their Carbon Footprint." *CBC*, 28 Feb. 2023, cbc.ca. Accessed 30 Nov. 2023.

8. "London Family Ditched the Suburbs."

9. Grace Smith. "Greta Thunberg Won't Attend COP27, Accusing It of 'Greenwashing.'" *Impakter*, 31 Oct. 2022, impakter.com. Accessed 30 Nov. 2023.

CARLA MOONEY

Carla Mooney is a graduate of the University of Pennsylvania. Today, she writes for young people and is the author of many books for young adults and children. Mooney enjoys reading about science and nature.